ADRIFT

A TALE OF SURVIVAL ON THE OCEAN

Nicole Fitzgerald

Presentation by *BookLeaf Publishing*

Web: www.bookleafpub.com

E-mail: info@bookleafpub.com

ISBN: 9789363311343

First edition 2024

Chapter 1: My Foolishness

On a beautiful Sunday afternoon, I set out with my family to enjoy some time on the water. Kayaking was a favourite pastime of ours, and we had recently equipped our daughter with her very own full-size one. I'd had my bright blue one for more than ten years.

After a quick look at the lake near our home, we decided there were too many powerboats and jet skis out so we headed to the beach instead. Not far from the carpark was an inlet that was nice and calm, and since it was relatively shallow, there were few, if any powered craft. We launched the 'yaks, settling into our life jackets and long sleeves and hats to protect us from the harsh Queensland sun. It was an absolutely beautiful afternoon. The water was glasslike and we spotted a few sea creatures beneath us as we paddled out.

I suppose it was a false sense of security or just a simply silly move, but I decided to go further out than I normally would. My kayak was gliding effortlessly across the water, and I wanted to paddle out past the rocks to check out the view. I glanced behind me and saw the other two were happily involved in a splash war, so I called out that I was paddling out a bit and my husband called back to be careful.

As I came around past the rocks into the current, I was surprised to find the previously slow-moving water morphing into a rapid rip tide. The surface was a lot rougher than I expected and I spent a good minute or two simply trying to keep balanced in my kayak. By the time I glanced up to orient myself, I was much further out to sea than I should have been. I could see my husband waving his paddle in the air but I could not hear his voice. I balanced my paddle on my legs and put both arms in the air to indicate that I was in trouble but there was simply no way for him to get to me. I was stuck fast in the riptide and being pulled away from shore very quickly.

Because there was no boat ramp near our inlet, and it was late on a Sunday afternoon, there was nobody near me on the water that I could call to for help. I was headed out to sea in a hurry but I knew better than to try and fight the current—instead, I floated for a few seconds to figure out exactly which direction I was being pulled in and then tried to paddle away from the current at a 90-degree angle, the idea being I would come out alongside the rip and could paddle back to the beach. This was the method I'd always heard to use while swimming, and I gave it my best shot as I mentally cursed my own foolishness. I tired quickly, and it became obvious that it was no use. I was stuck riding the current until it saw fit to spit me out.

I pulled my paddle out of the water and relaxed back into my seat, trying to conserve my energy. I knew once the rip exhausted itself I'd have to paddle all the way back and I was already feeling fatigued. I balanced my paddle across my legs to help me stay stable on the choppy water, and with every minute that passed my anxiety grew. There was still a good amount of time before darkness but I was on an unlit, unmotored, tiny little blue kayak. If I lost too much daylight it would be too easy for a bigger vessel to run me over, not seeing me so low on the water. I kept a watch around me hoping to find help and periodically looking over my shoulder. I could no longer see my loved ones, just the rocks at the end of the inlet. I knew my husband would be getting help so I tried to remain relaxed and patient while keeping vigilant for any indication I'd broken free of the rushing tide.

Every so often I would raise my paddle directly into the air and wave it, hoping that somewhere far behind me someone on shore had eyes on me.

The next ten minutes or so were more of the same. I was fighting anxiety as well as fatigue and my hope that help would miraculously pull up beside me was fading. The current did not seem to be abating so I decided it was time to try to break free again. I turned in the opposite direction from where I had tried earlier and gave it my all. Initially, I thought I was getting somewhere and hope bubbled up in my chest, only for a large wave to take me by surprise. Being side-on to oncoming waves in my kayak is never a good plan, given that it is designed for rivers and smooth waters, but being side-on and not looking was an even worse idea. Before I could gather my wits I was in the water, kayak upside down beside me.

The force of habit made me grab for the paddle before the water could carry it away, and then I righted my kayak. Because we often fish from our kayaks, we have bungee cords wrapped around different parts of the kayak, in case they are needed. I was so grateful for this, it meant I could tie my paddle to the kayak and I didn't have to worry about losing it while I battled to get back onboard. I swam around so the kayak and I were facing into the waves, and used my last vestiges of energy to drag myself onto it. It took several minutes and several rests but I made it back into my seat and sagged back against the drenched canvas.

When I got my breath back I tried to orient myself but I could no longer pick out the rocks. The waves were not breaking, but they were large enough that each one that passed was too high for me to see over. This was a bad sign—I knew I must be a long way out. Wearily, I unclipped my paddle and held it aloft for as long as I could. As I did, I tried to assess my situation realistically. The sun was setting and I did not have long before it would be dark. I couldn't see the shore, nor could I see any other landmarks so I did not know which direction I was heading in, but I decided to work under the theory that I was headed out in the same straight-ish line I had been since I got into trouble. Not ideal, considering it took me directly away from the shore, but not terrible. If I was headed straight out from the inlet sooner or later I would see the port, which was further around. If I kept alert, I could hopefully get some attention there. I knew my husband would have raised the alarm but given the circumstance, I didn't expect rescue until at least dawn. I was a tiny little speck in a very large ocean—even if the water police rallied everything they had, the chances of finding me in the dark were slim to none. My job was to stay afloat, stay alert, and hopefully make it through the night.

I then took an inventory of everything I had access to—kayak, paddle, life vest (oh thank god), long-sleeved shirt, singlet top, yoga pants, waterproof rubber shoes and six or so bungee cords (I only counted the ones I could see, although I was sure there were some attached behind my seat). Then the most wonderful realization hit me—there was a waterproof bag in the back storage compartment! We hadn't specifically packed for a longer trip because we only expected to be out for a couple of hours but that bag contained things like sunscreen, a small water bottle, and possibly a torch or reflector! The bags stay with the kayaks so it would be in the rear compartment, which with some contortion, I could theoretically reach from my seat. I tied the paddle up again so I wouldn't lose it in my enthusiasm and twisted and turned, trying to reach the round lid set into the surface of the kayak.

After a few minutes, I stopped, mindful of wasting too much energy. It would seem that with my canvas seat clipped on the way it was, it was physically not possible for me to reach the compartment. My arms were at least three inches too short. Usually, we'd pull the kayaks up alongside each other facing in opposite directions and access the compartment on the other person's kayak when we needed them on the water. I'd never tried to open the rear hatch, and realizing that I was unable to was a bitter disappointment. It meant that to get to it, I would need to deliberately hop into the water, swim to the back and then reboard once I'd retrieved the bag. I sat back in my seat and thought carefully. I couldn't be certain what was in the pack, but it would more than likely be something I could use. If I was really lucky it would be something I could use to signal, or possibly even a muesli bar or protein bar that I could eat to keep my energy up. The fact that I had finished my water a good couple of hours earlier and only had an empty bottle worried me, but I knew that the bag likely had a small bottle of water.

What was I to do? Sliding off the kayak into the water was fairly easy, if I was careful not to capsize it or lose the paddle. The water didn't feel cold when I put my hand in, but I knew deeper down it would be colder. I had no idea of depth, or underwater obstacles although I had the good shoes on so I would be protected from sharp rocks or reefs. Then there was the reboarding. It had taken a lot of energy earlier, and I was quite tired now. Plus, there was always the risk I might capsize accidentally again and I'd have to climb back—if I used all my energy now, would I even be able to?

I was still floating along but nowhere near the speed I had been going earlier. I was able to turn the kayak in a slow 360 to have a good look around me for boats, landmarks, planes or any other miracle that might happen. It was a circle of nothingness. All I could see in any direction was water. I was on my own.

Chapter 2: Easy Does It

I decided that it was only going to get later, and the low light was practically dark already so I would rest for a period, then try for the rear compartment. It didn't help that my night vision is quite poor and the time between the sun going down and total darkness is the worst time for me visually, at least when it's fully dark I can see lights and reflections. I decided to watch the stars for a bit—not that I'd ever been any good at celestial navigation, but I did like stargazing. After a few minutes of pondering the cosmos a shooting star shot across above me, so being superstitious, I made a wish that somehow, I would be okay.

Oddly that improved my spirits, so I decided to go for the bag. I made sure the paddle was secure, wrapped a couple of bungee ropes around my arm in case I needed them, took the deepest breath I've ever taken in my life and slipped off the relative safety of my kayak. The water was cold, but not unbearable, and the life vest did most of the work keeping me afloat. Hand over hand I worked my way to the rear of the kayak and screwed open the hatch. Inside was a sweet sight, a full-looking waterproof bag, sealed nice and tight. I tied it to the seat using one of the bungee ropes and then resealed the compartment. The temptation to empty out the bag and see what I'd won was overwhelming but I knew there'd be plenty of time for that—right now I had to focus on getting back on board. I contemplated unclipping the canvas seat for more manoeuvrability but ultimately decided my body needed the support it provided. I could always unclip it later.

I moved the bag to a spot where I'd be able to reach it but it wouldn't get in the way during my gymnastics, and then tried to haul myself back up. After three of the least graceful tries in my kayaking history, I was faced with a problem. I did not have enough strength in my arms and shoulders to pull myself up and across the kayak, meaning I could not get back on board.

Shit.

It wasn't a matter of resting and trying again. I was exhausted, and it was too great a task. I could have tied the kayak to my life vest and floated for a bit, but I was getting cold and the unknown darkness below me was unappealing. I had no way of knowing just how far out I was – had I passed the port already? – but I couldn't help thinking of all the creatures I was sharing the water with. Sharks, jellyfish, who knows what else. I needed a better plan.

Carefully I undid the bag and opened it up. I carefully put my hand in and rummaged around trying to identify the objects by feel. There was a travel-size tube, that'd be the sunscreen. A water bottle, what felt like a hand reel, something I couldn't identify and a plastic pouch of something. I pulled out the pouch and found protein balls. There were a couple more things I couldn't see in the very bottom but I decided the snack was what I needed. I re-tied the bag to the side of the kayak and had a small feast. As an added bonus, they were my favourite choc-mint-coconut flavour. Tucking the empty pouch into the front compartment, I relaxed back and floated alongside the kayak. I told myself that I was at home, curled up in the backyard with my dog watching the stars. I didn't want to sleep, I just wanted to recoup enough energy to get back on my kayak.

Then I heard it. At first, I thought it was my tired imagination, but nope—the whop-whop-whop of helicopter blades flying quite low. A second (third? fourth?) wind swept through me and on my second try I was able to haul myself over the kayak. I was trying to make as much commotion as I could to be as visible as possible as I wriggled around and righted myself on the kayak. My shaking hands untied the paddle as fast as I could and I started to wave it in the air. I could see an occasional flash in the sky and I hoped with everything I had that I'd be illuminated in a spotlight. I waved and screamed, calling as much attention to myself as I could but fatigue won out before I was spotted. I settled for holding the paddle across my lap and occasionally waving my arms. But the flash that accompanied the rhythmic sound was getting further away and tears of anger and futility spilled out of me.

After throwing myself a good pity party, I remembered the waterproof bag. If it was a search helicopter, that wouldn't be their only pass, and I'd be much more visible if I had a torch or something. I grabbed for the bag and dug through the contents but in the dark, it was difficult to tell what was what. Carefully, I rolled each item around in my hand, feeling for any clues, squinting in the dark at vague shapes. At the very bottom, I came across something that felt like a plastic bracelet, and I felt a searing pain in my heart thinking of my family, somewhere far behind me.

I pulled the bracelet out of the bag, hoping my daughter was warm and safe when I noticed an odd shimmer to the item. It wasn't a bracelet! It was reflective tape! I had to take a second to calm myself because it felt like there wasn't a great deal on the roll. How could I best use this? I could tape it onto the ends of the paddle, but it would only stay waterproof for so long and if the search took a few hours to find me I worried that it might simply wash off if I had to paddle. I could tape along the handle, but then friction from my hands might wear it off. If I was going to be out here for a few more hours I needed to use what I had as rationally as possible. Eventually, I carefully peeled off a few finger-lengths and, leaning forward as far as I could, I adorned the kayak with an X on either side, figuring the symbol for distress from my girl guide days was as good as any.

I put two more just behind my seat, as far back along the kayak as my hand would reach. The roll had some more on it so I peeled off about an inch and put it on the end of the paddle. The rest I would save for now. I rummaged around in the bag for the water bottle, and discovered another pack of protein balls. I put them aside for later and closed and re-tied the bag. I had felt the occasional sprinkle of what I thought might be rain, although it could just as easily be sea spray, so I wanted both my water bottles available to collect rainwater. I sipped from the smaller bottle and watched some clouds roll lazily overhead. No more shooting stars, but I was hoping for a different kind of moving light.

I can't believe it now, but I actually dozed off. I was propped up in the seat of the kayak with the paddle across my lap, and I was woken by a splash. I jerked upright, looking around for the rescuer I was sure had just landed nearby. It took a moment for my brain to realise I couldn't hear a helicopter overhead, nor were there any boats nearby. Another splash off the left side of the kayak made my blood run cold. It wasn't rescue. It was something unknown.

All of my senses were heightened in panic. Shark? Dolphin? Alien? I had no idea. I could barely see, I could just make out my own feet if I wiggled them, so I had to rely on my hearing. The splash had sounded close, and was on my left side. I stayed perfectly still and kept the paddle tightly in my hands, although the choppiness of the water made loud slapping sounds on the side of my kayak. I was a sitting duck. Another splash, this one behind me. Then one more on the left side. I was growing more and more fearful but not knowing what it was that was nearby meant I had no clue what action to take. I tried to remember anything I'd ever learned about sharks, but the only fact my terrified mind could recall was that they can smell blood in the water. I wasn't in the water, but I had been—was I bleeding? Had I cut or scratched myself somewhere in my efforts to reboard? I didn't know. I couldn't feel anything obvious but the cold water had made my exposed skin quite numb. All I could do was sit very still and wait.

I was straining my ears for another splash when the whop-whop-whop noise returned. This time I could see more than a flash, there was a helicopter flying very low over the water and a large beam of light sweeping back and forth. They were going to find me! Slowly, I raised the end of the paddle that had the tape on it as high as I could, careful not to make any noise that might aggravate my mysterious splasher. The light was swinging back and forth as the helicopter moved slowly over and it was getting closer and closer. I started to yell and scream, and waved the paddle with as much energy as I could muster. Any second now, any pass of that light is going to light up my reflective handiwork and then I'll be saved. Tears were streaming from my eyes again but this time they were tears of relief, of happiness. I was going home. I was going to be okay.

I vaguely heard another splash further away but I paid it no mind. My eyes were fixed firmly on that wonderful, lifesaving beam of light that I knew was going to fall on me. I was so certain of my impending rescue that it actually came as a shock when the beam started moving away. I was so stunned I couldn't move or speak. No! This isn't how it goes! They are turning around, they'll come back. They have to come back. I'm right here.

The helicopter started to move off, and to my utter horror, that beam of light disappeared. The sound of the helicopter blades faded into the distance as the reality of my situation hit me. I'd been missing for many hours by now, and they had a large area to search for my very small self. I knew they couldn't search indefinitely but surely they had a prediction of where I'd be, based on tides or currents or something? They must have a search area, and judging by the fact that all I could hear was the wind and the relentless water slapping, I was outside the search area. I had no way to navigate, no idea where I was, no way to get attention. I was on my own until daylight.

Too tired to cry, too overwhelmed to think, I sagged back into the seat looking in the direction the helicopter had gone. The thought crossed my mind that it would have to have come from land, perhaps I should paddle in the direction it had gone but the thought itself was exhausting, never mind fighting the sea to go in a direction based on a whim. I had to believe that they would be back, either tonight or at dawn. I had to hold on for just a few hours, I might be invisible in the dark but there would be boats out in the daylight.

I remembered my earlier plan to attract attention at the port and I realized I had not come across it in my semi-aimless floating. That meant I had likely deviated from the straight course; the riptide set me on at the mouth of the inlet. I could be anywhere. Then, a thought that scared me even more.

Where would I be when the sun rose?

Chapter 3: A Long Day

It was eerily peaceful for a while after that. I just sat, floating on my kayak. The water was calm enough, although the slap-slap-slap of waves against my kayak was ever-present. The sky was dark, starlit and cloudless. I couldn't see where the water ended and the sky began and my tiredness and stress began to meld into a dreamy, almost trance-like state. What was there to do? I couldn't see any sign of light around me, and was sure there were no other mariners stupid enough to be out in the ocean without any lights on. It was almost like being the only person on earth.

A cramping pain in my back reminded me that I was still in quite a dire situation. Everything might look peaceful but I might be headed straight for a rocky outcrop. I scanned the sky slowly and thoroughly and concluded that my paltry knowledge of the night sky meant that although beautiful, the starlit scene was navigationally useless to me. I kept reminding myself that the sun rises from the east, so when it showed itself I would—in theory—be able to paddle in the opposite direction to head west. I had been swept off the east coast of Australia, meaning that if I paddled far enough west I should bump into it. In theory. If I hadn't messed up entirely. For a few moments I became convinced that I was wrong, and the sun actually rose in the west, so I'd need to paddle east. Geography, much like not doing stupid things like paddling into a rip current, has never been my strong suit.

I'm a creative type. In my head I could see what inspired Van Gogh, I could picture Shakespeare staring up at the sky. I could even remember the opening to a sonnet:

Not from the stars do I my judgement pluck,
And yet methinks I have astronomy
But not to tell of good or evil luck
Of plagues, dearths or seasons' quality.

Had I pen and paper, I could have written my own poetry about the situation I found myself in. The ethereal beauty of the night sky with zero light pollution was majestic. I could see the Milky Way streaking across the sky and the stars themselves seemed alive—twinkling, shimmering, sparkling.

But instead of words and rhymes, I was out here in the cold with a paddle and a sore back. My normal talents were of no use to me. I thought it through carefully and decided that I was right the first time, the sun rose in the east and set in the west. So once it was visible in the sky, I would paddle with it to my back. I was hungry, thirsty, tired and alone. I had to keep going until I could see the sun. Then, I would power my weary body with thoughts of home.

Somewhere amongst the rhythm of the water against the side of my kayak, and the deafening silence of the night sky, I must have dozed. I was smart enough to wrap a bungee cord around the paddle and attach it to my life vest just in case, and I'm glad I did. I was pretty much up the proverbial creek and my only advantage was the paddle. I didn't wake up, so much as become gradually aware that the sky was getting lighter. If I had slept, it was a light snooze at best. I could see nothing but water, with the occasional bird flying high above me. At one point in the predawn light, I could have sworn vultures were circling but I think I might have sleepily misidentified a couple of curious seagulls.

My mystery splasher didn't come back, but not long after the sun hit the horizon I became aware of a shape that appeared and receded alongside me. For a while I didn't move, just watching the underwater shadow come and go until it broke the surface and revealed itself to be a dolphin. I recalled stories from sailors who had been rescued by dolphins, and the theory that the myth of mermaids had been borne of stranded sailors who had been befriended by dolphins but this one just seemed curious. I couldn't see if there was more than one but he came and went. As the sun got higher in the sky, I stretched as best I could and readied myself for a hard day of paddling. I ate the other pack of protein balls, savouring the sweet flavour. I did not know how the day would go, but I was reasonably certain that between my heading west and the search and rescue, I'd be home by nightfall.

My dolphin friend would appear next to me for a bit, then disappear. I christened him Bob because of his way of bobbing up beside the kayak. The day was brightening up and I estimated it to be around 5 am. I was more alert now, watching for the sun, paddling in slow circles to warm up my muscles. I thought about my husband and my daughter, I pictured them happily splashing as I'd seen them yesterday. I hoped they were safe somewhere and not too afraid for me. After all, aside from not knowing where I was, there wasn't much wrong with me. No injuries, my kayak was sound, although, perhaps not ideal for the conditions and in the light of day it seemed ludicrous that I would be lost in the middle of the ocean.

I was off the coast of Queensland, Australia. People knew I was missing, there had been a search last night. There was likely a search getting underway, if not already underway right now. Any time now, I would see a boat or helicopter, I could wave my paddle and they'd see me in the daylight. I had company, thanks to Bob, and as we waited in the sun I started talking to him. I told him all about my family, about how my daughter would be terribly jealous that I had made his acquaintance because of her fondness for animals. I told him what I should be doing at home on that Monday morning. He was good company, and it seemed like he was listening to me ramble.

The sun rose, as it has every day since the beginning of time, but never before has there been a sunrise like it. The purple of the night slowly faded into a pink, then orange, and there it was. I watched the day being born with a ridiculous grin on my face. Lost? I wasn't really lost. I was on an unexpected adventure! Hadn't I seen enough artistic inspiration for the rest of my life in the sky last night? And now, to be watching this so-called everyday miracle. I stretched my hands and arms and loosened my shoulders. It was time to paddle home so I could tell my daughter how beautiful the world is.

My delight and joy at the sight of the rising sun lasted a fair while, the paddling was easy and I got into a slow rhythm by reciting song lyrics and poems in my head. I felt that I must be making good time. The kayak was skimming over the water almost as easily as it had the day before at the inlet. I entertained visions of me riding the waves heroically, landing on the beach and stepping off my kayak in front of a worried crowd with an air of smug calm. Me? Lost? Don't be silly. I just wanted to see the stars.

After I'd been paddling for at least two hours I thought I might turn around and see how far up the sun was. I swung the kayak around in a lazy arc so I was facing the opposite direction and stopped short. It had barely moved. It was still almost on the horizon, surrounded by pinks and oranges. My "at least" two hours of paddling was half an hour at best. There were still no landmarks around me so I had no idea how far I'd come. My visions of rockstar cool arrivals on the beach evaporated in the early morning heat and I came down off my temporary high. This wasn't a joke, or an adventure. I couldn't play this off as just a minor mistake. Taking several deep breaths to calm my pounding heart, I slowly turned my back to the sun and started paddling again. I kept up the slow constant paddling, knowing that wearing myself out this early in the day was dangerous. Song lyrics and poems deserted me and instead, I had a mantra. I want to go home. I want to go home. I want to go home.

It occurred to me some time into the morning that I hadn't seen my dolphin friend since I started paddling, and I felt a little sad. Any company was better than absolutely none. At what I thought was about 10 am, I reached up to wipe sweat off my face and realized I was getting burnt. I was sure I'd had a hat, but after thinking a bit, I realized I must have lost it when I capsized the day before. I found the sunscreen in the waterproof bag and applied it generously all over my face, ears, neck and hands. The rest of me was covered in sunproof clothing. Idly, I thought how well-prepared we thought we were for being out on the water, with our life vests and sun protection. We prided ourselves on being responsible. I didn't feel very proud or responsible right then.

I picked up my water bottle for another sip and was disheartened to discover it was almost my last. I still had the larger bottle, but it was empty. All I could do was hope for rescue, or failing that, rain.

There wasn't much to think about, other than paddling. I sang for a while, simply because I got sick of the noise of the water. After I'd gone through my repertoire of Christmas Carols and lullabies, I ran out of things to sing, so I started telling myself terrible jokes. After a while I lapsed back into silence and stared at the horizon. My tired mind pondered where I might go—would I wash up on a beach in New Zealand? Or would I freeze to death by going too far south? The sky was that brilliant blue that Queenslanders know so well, without a hint of cloud. I tried to tell myself that it would be easier to spot rescue but all I could think about was how hot and sweaty I was, and how that was going to get worse as the day rolled on. I knew better than to take off my long-sleeved shirt. I'm one of those delightfully pale people that can get sunburned indoors. I'd fry in minutes out here.

So I sweated, and paddled, and mumbled to myself. I want to go home. I want to go home. I want to go home. I could feel the sun's heat on my back, and an image of Dory from Finding Nemo popped into my head. Just keep swimming! That was slightly more positive. So with each stroke, I heard her cartoon voice in my head singing *just keep paddling, just keep paddling....*

Just. Keep. Paddling.

Chapter 4: Paradise Found

The sun reached its highest point, and I decided it was time for a rest. I wasn't sure how many hours I had been paddling for but I needed a stretch and a break. I drained the final drops of my water, and scanned the sky for any sight of a cloud. Usually, I love the sight of a blue cloudless sky, although usually I'm not this desperate for a sign of fresh water. I had both my bottles wedged beside my leg, ready at the first sign of rain. I was starting to get uncomfortably hungry and I could feel the beginnings of a headache at my temples.

Since the water was relatively calm, I opened the waterproof bag and began a thorough inventory. Reflective tape, very little. Hand reel, with a small hook tied onto the end. One packet of choc-orange protein balls, empty. Tube of sunscreen, just under half-full. Plastic bag of small fishing hooks containing two good hooks and one broken one. Half a protein ball, rock hard and stale and covered in all manner of things. At the very bottom, I discovered a bright orange whistle. I gave it a try and was pleasantly surprised at how loud it was. That discovery was immediately clipped to the life vest. The bottom of the bag had some little crumbs and debris in it but no other items. It was wide at the top when fully open, and I thought it might be easier to catch water in than a water bottle. I carefully washed it out with sea water and clipped it to the side of the kayak to dry. Still no sign of rain but I felt better knowing I was prepared if any should come along.

The sunscreen, fish hooks and hand reel I tucked into the hollow under my knees. If I capsized ,I would lose them but it was a risk I was willing to take to have the bag available to catch fresh water. I looked for a while at the stale half protein ball but couldn't bring myself to eat it. I ended up tucking it in the plastic bag with the fish hooks—I doubted many fish would be interested in it but since I had no other bait it was worth saving. I carefully examined every area I could see. I knew there was nothing in the forward compartment of the kayak—it was more of an access point to the interior of the kayak and so storing anything in there was impossible. I had no pockets on my pants, and the pocket on my shirt was empty. Patting myself down, I discovered a small mesh pocket on the front of the life vest—inside was a tiny little pencil torch. I was excited for all of thirty seconds until I discovered it was well and truly dead. Still, I replaced it in the pocket.

I made sure all the various items were tucked away as safe as I could get them, then reapplied sunscreen. The sun was now shining directly onto my face and I cursed the loss of my hat. I picked up the paddle and after a stretch and a good look around, resumed my slow and steady pace. The break had done me good and after a few minutes I started to speed up a little. I wanted to get as far as I could in the hopes of running into a rescue effort. The lack of landmarks or indeed anything to see was wearing my spirit down. There was just water, in all directions. Every ten or so strokes, I would raise my head and scan around and after paddling for an indeterminate amount of time, I saw a shape way off to my right. It looked like a large ship, although from where I was sitting it was tiny. My heart jumped but I knew there was no way I could make it to the shape, nor be seen by it. It was too far away. It was comforting however, being the first sign of other humans I had seen in so many hours.

It looked to be heading east, although I couldn't be completely certain. That validated my plan to keep moving west, so I kept up the faster pace. Dory was long gone and instead I was counting strokes—one-and-two-and-three-and-four, and-one-and-two-and-three-and-four. My arms and shoulders were not feeling too bad but I knew they would hurt later on.

As the afternoon wore on, the water started to get rougher. First, I noticed that the slapping against the side had become slapping over the side, and then gradually I was aware of the nose of the kayak dipping into the lull between waves, then cresting the next one. Paddling was not as easy now, so I slowed my efforts and went back to the steady rhythm of the morning. I glanced into the sky and was pleasantly surprised to see patches of cloud. Perhaps, it would rain after all. Soon, I had to stop paddling and focus more on keeping myself upright. The water was no longer calm, and the waves were growing in size. The wind had also picked up and was coming from somewhere in front of me, meaning when I was head-on into the wind all I could hear was a whooshing noise.

The situation was becoming concerning, and I wondered whether I should turn back and seek out calmer waters. The sky had darkened, although I could still make out the sun, but it looked as if a rain squall (or worse!) was building. My kayak was not designed for this type of water. I was at serious risk of capsizing, and quite possibly not being able to recover—or possibly losing what precious few items I had.

After a moment's indecision, I decided things looked calmer out to my left, so I started a diagonal change of direction. I was not risking taking these waves side on.

Slowly, timing my paddling carefully, I worked my way diagonally to the left of where I had been. I knew it was taking me off course, but what good was being on course if I drowned? I felt fatigue start to make itself known, and the splashes of water against my face were no longer pleasantly cooling, rather they were like being slapped and often I would have to stop to wipe my eyes. As I was concentrating on trying to predict the approaching waves, I felt a steady drip from above, which quickly developed into a shower. The rain I had wished for so fervently was here, but I was in no position to take advantage of it.

Miserable, soaked, demoralized and thoroughly disoriented, I just kept my head low and tried to paddle on the rise of each wave, then ride over the top of it. I had to stay upright, and I had to keep moving. At one point, there was a slight lull and I was able to quickly rearrange my waterproof bag so it was open to the sky. I knew it would likely catch the splashing seawater as well but it was better than nothing.

The rainfall got heavier, and the waves got larger. I abandoned my diagonal trajectory and just focused on taking each wave as it came, trying my best to hit nose-first to avoid capsizing. I was pretty much holding onto the paddle for dear life and passively trying to ride out the rough seas. A couple of times I spotted something off to the left, but never a good enough look to identify it. Driftwood? Rocks? Some kind of large piece of flotsam? It didn't matter, I couldn't get to it. I just rode the waves like some kind of involuntary roller coaster, with the water bottles firmly between my knees and the waterproof bag clipped to the side. I hoped I was catching some water. The thirst would have been unbearable if I wasn't so distracted by what felt like imminent drowning.

I saw a particularly high wave coming. I knew I would have to hit it properly or it would be all over. I angled the nose of the kayak and waited… and rode the wave up to its height. I hadn't realized I'd been holding my breath but I exhaled sharply as my kayak balanced on the wave. Suddenly, I could identify that vague colour off to my left. It was a fair way away, but it was a sandbank! That was almost land!! Now, I had a plan. I was going to move slowly left with each passing wave. The water around the sandbank looked calmer, and it seemed to be acting as a wave break.

I timed each wave with a precision I didn't know I was capable of. I messed up a couple of times, and came perilously close to capsizing once, but slowly, achingly slowly, I made my way towards my oasis. I couldn't tell you how long it actually took, but it felt like days. Gradually the waves were getting less like a roller coaster and more like little speed bumps. I didn't dare look at the sandbank beyond simple navigation—I could examine it when I was closer. Every so often I would check that I was headed in the right direction and finally, it was within reach and the water was calm enough that I could get a proper look without putting myself at risk.

It wasn't much. It was a sandbank in the very basic sense of the word. There wasn't a friendly palm tree or a castaway from some other misadventure waving in welcome. It was simply a stretch of sand. To me, it looked like paradise.

The sea was cooperating, and I was getting closer and closer, until a very welcome bump as the front of my kayak beached itself. I pushed myself as far up the sand as I could with the paddle to ensure I was secure, and then sagged back into my seat. The rain was light but steady, so I checked the waterproof bag and decided the inch or so of water in the bottom was likely mostly seawater. I tipped it out and then positioned it so it was filling with precious fresh rainwater. The bottles I had between my knees had collected about a sip between them, so I wedged them near the waterproof bag and secured them with a bungee cord. I did not have the strength in me to climb out of the kayak. My legs had started to shake and my upper body was stiff and sore, so I just sat in my kayak, still for the first time in about 24 hours.

I did not know if the sandbar was tidal or whether it was always above the water. There were no plants or other clues, but there was a line a bit further up that seemed to be a high tide line—a collection of bits of seaweed, sticks and other debris. Once I had rested, I could pull the kayak above that line and lay on the sand for a bit.

I don't know how long I sat there letting the rain wash over me and the sea rage around me, but eventually, I looked up to the sky to see that it was getting on towards sunset. That motivated me to carefully and slowly climb out of the kayak. I immediately collapsed, my legs weak and unbalanced, but I crawled up to the front of the kayak and dragged it to the highest point of the sandbar. I wished there was something I could tether it to but decided I'd just tether it to myself and that would have to do. I tied the paddle across the kayak and collapsed alongside it.

I'd made it to land, possibly collected some water, and I wouldn't (hopefully) have to spend another night atop a black and unknown ocean. It was some time before my thoughts turned to the search and rescue I had been hoping for, and I took comfort in the fact that my bright blue kayak would stand out against the beige of the sandbar. I took two bungee cords and bound the kayak to my wrist and my ankle, curled up and let exhaustion sweep me into unconsciousness.

I was safe, I hoped, for now at least.

Chapter 5: Hunger Games

I awoke to early morning light, having slept fitfully through the night. Aside from raging thirst and hunger, I felt better. The rain had stopped sometime after I fell asleep and I hoped it had continued long enough to give me a supply of water. After taking some time to fully wake up I untied the bungee rope around my wrist and then the one around my ankle, and moved up to the end of the kayak where my water-catching rig was set up. I was pleased to see the waterproof bag was over half full, and each of the bottles had at least an inch of water. I had to stop myself from drinking it all immediately. I picked up the small bottle and sat back down on the sand, sipping the rainwater and looking around me. Much like the day before it was just ocean in all directions, although I felt that I was better off today given the refuge of the sandbar. When I had finished the water in the bottle, I submerged it in the waterproof bag, allowing it to fill. I then poured it into the bigger bottle and sealed it. Carefully, I tried to pour what was in the bag into the smaller bottle but I spilled some, and so rather than waste it I simply drank it out of the bag.

Refreshed and quenched, I stood up to explore my surroundings. It seemed I had been right about the tide line, meaning that not counting storms or unusual weather, most of the sandbar was exposed at all times. As I walked the length of the sand I saw that there was actually quite a bit of seaweed and other debris, and it would be possible for me to make a large mark or message in the hopes of being seen by someone overhead. I stood at the edge of the sandbar and looked around me slowly, hoping for even a small sign of land but could see nothing. I refused to allow myself to be disappointed—I had made it through more than a day stranded out here, and I had found my way to a piece of dry land. I was doing okay in the scheme of things.

While the sun was still low and the day was cool I decided two things needed to happen—I needed to make some kind of sign on the sand that would be very obvious to anyone flying over, and I needed to see if there was any way to make a kind of shelter from the sun. I had, perhaps, one application's worth left of sunscreen, and then I was at the mercy of the sun. I began by taking my life vest off and laying it in the kayak. I took off my long-sleeved shirt and stretched it out across the kayak, weighing it down with the bottle of water in the hopes it would dry at least a little before the sun got too high. Now dressed only in a singlet and pants I was a little cold, so I started to move quickly around the sandbar collecting seaweed, shells, rocks and anything else I could find. I made a pile in the centre and as I worked I warmed up quite quickly. After my third circle around the edge of the sandbar, I was confident I had everything. I went to the pile and started sorting it into smaller piles so I could see what I had. The seaweed and sticks would be the most useful, as they were of the darkest colours. I needed things that could be seen from a large distance and the white shells and light-coloured rocks would help in keeping things together but not in visibility.

I looked over the sandbar critically and decided the narrower end opposite to where I had beached my kayak was where I would work. I couldn't decide if I should write "HELP" or try to make a symbol, and after a short period of indecision, I decided a large arrow would look unnatural enough to gather attention, and be easier to construct. Starting close to the tide line, I made a thick line of seaweed for about a metre, then used the sticks, rocks and other debris to form the arrow. I then took a thick stick I'd left aside and started to dig an indent around the arrow. I did everything I could think of to make it visible, and by the time I was done, the sun was starting to beat down uncomfortably. I looked at my morning's work and was satisfied that the large arrow, pointing directly at my bright blue kayak, was sufficient.

Next on the agenda was some kind of shelter. I picked up my still-wet long-sleeved shirt and put it back on, but instead of buttoning it up I just tied it at my waist. It would protect my arms and shoulders but hopefully I wouldn't be as hot. I looked at the kayak, and the sandbar itself, and realized that the arrow had been a piece of cake compared to this task. How was I going to make shelter? I had nothing to lean the kayak on or tilt it against, and it was the only piece of construction material I had. Wearily I sank down beside it. Could I construct a makeshift tent out of my clothing? No, I decided, it was better to wear them for protection. I decided the kayak was my only choice, and set about unclipping the canvas seat and gathering all the items stashed in various places. Once I had stripped the kayak of all extra items, I tried to turn it on its side to act as a shade. I tried various ways, including digging a small trench to sit it in, but try as I might I couldn't get it to do anything other than sit upright or upside down, neither of which was very useful. The paddle I had dug into the sand so it was standing upright (with the small patch of reflective tape uppermost, of course). I refused to allow myself the luxury of wishing I had this item or that, instead focusing on what I did have.

After some time, I was hot and exhausted, and so I decided to put shelter aside for now and have a bit of a break while I worked on my next move. I had the tiniest sip of water from the bottle, and put all the items back into the kayak. I picked up the seat and had an idea. After several minutes of fiddling, I managed to tie it to the paddle so it was shaped like an inverted L, and provided a small square of shade—just enough for my head. In case I fell asleep again, I tethered myself to the kayak once more, then wriggled under my makeshift shade. I could feel the sun almost directly overhead, and was grateful that the only exposed skin I had was a couple of inches between my pants and shoes. My hands were underneath my head acting as a pillow, and I figured I might as well try to rest, but listen out for any passing boats or aircraft.

My mind wandered to where I might be. I had not heard or seen any sign of anyone all day, not even a bird. Oddly, I wasn't particularly lonely, just focused. I had to stay alive, because I had to get home. So I didn't entertain maudlin thoughts of what ifs or wishes for rescue as I had on the first night. Everything was about the here and now. If rescue came I would do everything I could to attract their attention but if they didn't I would not let the sea defeat me. My plan was to spend the night where I was, and start again to the west when the sun came up the next day. I did have niggling doubts, thinking that perhaps I was safer where I was, but that would inevitably circle around to not knowing where I was, and if I didn't know where I was, would anyone else? After a while of back and forth I decided that in the immortal words of Scarlett O'Hara: "I won't think about that today, I'll think about that tomorrow."

I wriggled around until I had a comfortable little dent in the sand, and tried to nap. I was comfortable enough, but the ache in my belly was becoming unignorable. My thoughts turned to that stale, half protein ball, but it seemed like that would only make things worse. If I were to use it to bait the hand reel and try to fish, that could work, but my knowledge of fishing was limited to fishing in rivers with my husband, whose knowledge far surpassed mine in species, whether they were safe to eat and even how to prepare and cook them. That brought up another thought—I had a nice collection of Girl Scout badges from my youth but not one of them was survival or camping or anything that might be useful now. I could help the elderly, I was an excellent reader and I could repair a torn item of clothing in a pinch. More skills that did me no good stranded on a patch of sand in the middle of the ocean.

I was surprised to find that despite my resolve I was still holding out hope to be rescued by nightfall, which seemed a little ridiculous given how many hours it had been since I had seen a rescue attempt. I was confident I had done my best to make myself visible with the arrow pointing at the kayak, and unease began to creep through me as I imagined the rescue helicopter seeing my sign only to find me dead on the sand. Somewhere deep in memory, I recalled someone telling me fish were more likely to bite at night. That would be an interesting endeavour given my poor night vision, but if I baited the hook with a little bit of protein ball while it was still light, it might be worth a go.

What I would do with a fish if I caught it—well that was something I'd worry about later. I moved out of my little shade and stood up. I did my now customary scan of all directions and wasn't surprised or saddened when I saw nothing. It was what I had come to expect. Next, I walked to each edge of the sandbar, trying to work out if it was gradual on all sides or if there was a drop-off into deeper water. On the opposite side to the side I had beached on, it seemed to go into the water for about half a metre and then drop off. Carefully, I made my way down the slope into the water, to where it suddenly got deeper. This looked like a good spot to sit and throw a line in. I figured I may as well, having the line and all, it's not like I had a million things to do otherwise.

I stood as still as a statue and watched, hoping to spot a fish—any fish. A small piece of seaweed washed up onto my feet but that was all. I picked it up and added it to my arrow. I spent some time idly making the indent around it a little deeper and wider, adjusting a piece of seaweed or a rock here and there. I heard a couple of small plop-splash noises, which made me hopeful there were fish who might be interested in a protein ball snack a bit later, and made my way over to the kayak to bait up my hook. I took a moment to mentally send thanks to my husband. I have never been able to tie hooks onto my lines, so he always does it for me and we leave my handreels equipped with hooks. I felt a familiar stab of pain at the thought of him, but was immediately distracted by the hook stabbing me in the thumb. It was a good thing, as I couldn't afford those emotions right now. I did my best to bait the hook with some tiny morsels, then stowed it in the kayak.

I glanced up at the sky to see clouds forming similar to the day before. I quickly set up the waterproof bag and the empty bottle, hopeful I'd get another bounty overnight. Then, I laid down next to the shade so I could watch the sky for a bit, or move over under the shade if I needed to. I saw a lone seagull making lazy circles, and some fluffy white clouds drifting slowly by. The sky was getting darker as the sun moved further down toward the horizon, and after a while a very light rain began to fall. I shifted under my improvised shelter and closed my eyes.

I pictured my husband and daughter, not scared or stressed as I knew they would be now, but happy. Stretching out their arms to welcome me back. I imagined one of my daughter's violently enthusiastic hugs that she gives when we've been apart, and my husband's strong arms around my shoulders.

Then I told myself it was rain streaking down my face, and rolled over to curl up on my side and try to remember everything I knew about fishing. In a couple of hours, I was going to undertake the most practical exam ever.

I was either going to pass, or die trying.

Chapter 6: So Close

The rain continued at a steady pace for a while and then started to increase. It rapidly changed from a sprinkle to a downpour, and I moved out from under my shelter to investigate. To my dismay, the sky was thick with dark clouds and it appeared I was right underneath a developing storm. I looked all around and the sea had turned dark and rough, and I was right in the middle of things. I started to panic, wringing my hands and staring dumbly at the rain pounding down onto the kayak when I was pulled from my freakout by a rumble. The unmistakable rumble of a thunderstorm.

Panic was replaced by anger. Pure rage surged through my veins and I yelled to nowhere in particular that I wasn't beaten yet, if Mother Nature wanted me dead, she had a fight on her hands. I emptied the waterproof bag into the bottles as best I could, spilling plenty but not caring. I gathered up all the little objects—the sunscreen and handreel, the hooks, loose bungee cords, and anything else I could cram into the bag and then I sealed it up tight, returning it to the rear compartment. I didn't like the idea of it being inaccessible again but I liked the idea of losing it even less, so in it went. I untied the seat from the paddle and clipped it back onto the kayak, and put my life jacket back on. I looked wildly around to ensure nothing was loose or left abandoned, then I climbed aboard my kayak and held the paddle across my knees. I had no intention of launching, rather I was prepared for an inadvertent departure if the seas got too high. I had no shelter from the wild wind and rain, and while I could hear rumbles around me I had not seen any lightning yet. The seas all around me were becoming more violent, the waves topped with white, and every so often a large wave would crash into the sandbar.

I hunkered into my seat and relaxed my legs. I would occasionally stretch my toes and rotate my ankles. I knew if I was launched involuntarily, I would have to fight to stay upright, and that meant bracing myself into the footholds firmly. Bracing for long periods inevitably brought leg cramps, so I wanted my muscles warm and loose. Ideally, I would have liked to turn the kayak so I faced the water directly but it being lodged in the sand meant I would have to climb out to do so, and I truly thought that a wave big enough to carry the kayak away could hit anytime, so I stayed put.

With the loudest crack I had ever heard the sky directly in front of me lit up with a bolt of lightning that branched out across the sky. It was awe-inspiring, and terrifying at the same time. I kept my paddle horizontal across my legs and tried to make myself as small as possible. I knew I was the highest point, which meant danger but I didn't know what to do about it. I hoped that my weight on top of the kayak would keep it on whatever remained of the sandbar, but I was also prepared to do battle with the sea. Lightning, I couldn't do much about. I ignored the rumbles, cracks and flashes and instead kept a wary eye around me. I could not work out which direction the tide was going, as it all seemed to be heading for me.

The rain kept falling, seemingly inexhaustibly. I drank my fill directly from the sky and filled both bottles. I wished I had the bag to fill as well, but it was better off where it was. At least with everything else going on, I had managed to slake the terrible thirst. Another loud crack made it sound like the sky was coming apart at the seams. I didn't look, instead watching the sea and started to sing bits of songs I could remember that had the word 'rain' in them. On my third attempt at 'It's Raining Men', I realized the rumbling was getting less frequent, and a bit quieter. I hadn't heard any cracks in a while so I risked a look. The sky was still dark and ominously cloudy but there was a shift I couldn't quite articulate. It was still raining heavily, the wind was still trying to steal the paddle from my hands, but there was a sort of calmness in the air.

Immediately my mind rushed to the conclusion that this was the eye of the storm, and worse was to come. I started Phil Collin's 'Rain Down On Me,' figuring that if it was going to get worse there was nothing I could do about it anyway. My singing got louder and angrier. All I had wanted to do was enjoy an afternoon outdoors with my family, and now I was going to die in the middle of the ocean. What did I ever do to deserve this fate?

Singing turned to arguing. I began to question why the storm existed, why I was caught in it, why I even existed. I screamed insults and challenges to the flashing sky, shouting that the lightning wasn't brave enough to strike me. I was done with the entire situation. I had my face to the sky, eyes shut, when I was surprised by a sudden ceasing of the downpour. I blinked in surprise, and looked up.

The clouds were receding. The heavy blackness was gone, replaced by puffs of what I thought were white clouds and patches of dark. I stared in surprise and wonder. Had I really just waited out an actual storm? Out to the right of me, I could see a patch of what I now recognized as the night sky. The storm had lasted all afternoon, and I had somehow made it through. I mentally shook myself, and took stock of my surroundings. The kayak was fine, just slightly waterlogged. I still had the paddle, and everything on me. The compartments were watertight meaning I still had all my things. I had two full and sealed bottles of fresh water. The sandbar was still just as it had been, the waves were no longer hitting my kayak. I looked back up at the sky and I could see the odd star peeking through the cloud cover.

I sat silently, thankfully, aware that I had added another incredible survival to my already impressive list. I couldn't believe that I, the girl who shied away from things that were too real and preferred to live a life of fiction and make-believe, was surviving whatever nature threw at me based solely on my own wits. And luck, of course. Boatloads of luck.

I was smiling wryly at the idea of a kayak-load of luck when I noticed something about the sandbar stretching out in front of me.

There was no sign whatsoever of my carefully crafted arrow.

I felt nothing. I wasn't distressed that it had been washed away, I wasn't happy. I just accepted it, and slowly lifted a leg off the side of the kayak. I got up carefully, and stood on the sand looking around me. I couldn't see any lights or anything to grab my attention. I finished my slow scan and looked at the sky again. It looked calm enough. I had a sore throat from my crazy shouting and singing, and I suddenly felt down-to-my-bones weary. Not just tired from the day, although I certainly was, but weary of everything. I didn't set up the paddle and seat shelter, or even take off my life vest. I just lay down in the sand and stared out at the waves. During the drama, I was brave and strong, but in the calm moments, I was a mess of fear and regret.

After a long time, I saw a shape moving out of the water. A golden light surrounded it, and I raised my head to look. My daughter was climbing the sandbank with her arms outstretched. I could see my husband behind her, our dog at his side. She was reaching for me and calling to me in her sweet voice. I was saved. I pushed myself off my sandy bed and moved towards her. Her smile soothed my fractured and fearful heart, and the golden light looked warm and comforting. She was so close, I just had to reach out and she would take my hand. I reached out for the haven of my family.

I was brought rudely back to reality by the chill of the water. I had indeed moved off the sand, and was standing knee-deep in the cold, dark ocean. I screamed and collapsed to my knees. They had been so close.

After the bitterness subsided, I felt the water moving around me with little splashes. I felt drained of everything—energy, motivation, the will to fight. But I knew I had to keep going—just keep paddling!—because my baby girl and my beloved were waiting for me. The golden light had been nothing but a hallucination but I was reminded that there was more at stake here than just my life. I had to keep going so I could see them again for real. Even if I collapsed in their arms and never moved again, I would see them for real. I stood and moved out of the chilly water. I was wide awake, so I needed a task to keep myself moving. Not far from where I had been standing was the point where the sandbar dropped off into deeper waters. It was time to go fishing.

I discarded the life jacket into the kayak and grabbed the handreel. I put the packet of extra hooks (and a crumbled protein ball) into the pocket of my shirt and buttoned it up. I closed my eyes and tried to picture what my husband had told me about casting a line by hand,—he was always so much better at it than I—asked the sea for some mercy, and cast it. My first attempt was dismal. The line caught around itself and fell two feet in front of me. I gathered it in and tried again. The second cast was better, it sailed several metres. The hook had a tiny metal ball tied on top between it and the line. I thought it was called the sinker but couldn't remember, in any case, I should have been using a bigger one. I let it lay for a moment and then slowly wound it back up onto the reel.

I repeated this performance over and over. I didn't get so much as a nibble. After every few casts, I would check to make sure the hook still had some bait. After my seventeenth unsuccessful cast, I checked the hook and discovered I was missing some. This was a development. I pulled the bag out of my shirt pocket and rebaited the hook, then cast in the same direction. This time I wound slower. I still felt no nibbles, but when I got the hook all the way in I had no bait left at all.

Either I had a bite, or I was dragging the hook against something that was making the bait fall off. I rebaited and cast. This time I didn't wind it in. I just waited. I held the line with the greatest of care and attention. Was that a nibble? I could feel a tiny vibration through the line. I made myself wait until the tiny vibration became a noticeable tug.

I pulled the line in quickly. There, dangling at the very end of my line, was a small and rather unimpressed-looking crab. I could have sworn it gave me a dirty look before letting go and dropping back into the water. Much further out across the water, the moon had come out and was making the tops of the water sparkle like jewels. It looked to be one or two days off being full. I stared at it for a while before carefully winding up the handreel and tucking the hook in safely.

I glanced at the sand next to my kayak but couldn't face sleep yet. I knew I would just ruminate over all the things I couldn't do. Instead, I set about gathering what I could to make another arrow. There wasn't nearly as much seaweed as there had been, so I used the paddle to dig a furrow in the sand and then piled whatever I could find into that. I ended up with a pretty decent-looking arrow, at least in the moonlight. I put my life vest down as a pillow and lay on my back on the sand. I closed my eyes and tried to lose myself in happy memories, telling myself that surely I'd be found tomorrow.

Definitely tomorrow.

Chapter 7: Gone

I awoke late, to the squawk of seagulls overhead. Forgetting where I was for a moment, I watched them wheel around on the breeze, almost as if they were flirting with each other. Around and around they went, circling and diving, and then off they flew. I felt inspired and hopeful. Today would absolutely be the day I was found, or that I found myself. I smiled and my hope wasn't even daunted by the sunburn I could feel on my face. I sat up and reached into the kayak to find the sunscreen and applied the last of it to my burnt skin. How my daughter would laugh at my sunburn after all the times I'd scolded her for going out with her fair skin unprotected! The sun was already well overhead but that was alright, it just made it easier to follow. I would take my time, pack everything up and head west to find home.

Packing was quicker than I anticipated but I couldn't shake the feeling that something was missing. I checked, rechecked, then emptied the waterproof bag and checked again. Sunscreen (empty), handreel, spare hooks and bait, reflective tape, water bottles – it was all there. My life vest was on the seat, and I was wearing all of my clothing. Hands on hips I stood and contemplated my lot. It all seemed complete, so eventually, I decided I was just tired after everything. I loaded the waterproof bag into the rear compartment, checked that the seat was securely clipped in and wriggled the kayak to a suitable launch position. I put my life vest on and adjusted the clips, which seemed a lot looser than they had a couple of days ago. I reached for my paddle so I could set off …

My paddle.

My paddle was gone.

Frantically, I tried to remember the last time I had seen it. It had been late last night, in the moonlight. I had used it to scoop a narrow trench in the sand to make my arrow. I walked over to the pitiful scratchings I had been so proud of the night before and retraced my steps. I had made the mark in the sand, then put the paddle down beside me so I could stretch the seaweed along its length. Already knowing what I would see and feeling a little sick, I turned to where I had put the paddle down the night before. My sturdy, strong-but-lightweight paddle, designed to float in almost all conditions. I had set it down beside me, about a foot below the tide line that marked where the tides had peaked in the early morning before I had awoken.

Of course, it was gone. It was designed and manufactured to be lighter than water, and to float gracefully. As soon as the tide started to recede from the sandbar, it would have floated atop it. My paddle would be somewhere out there, in the great expanse of the ocean. I had no hope of finding it, let alone retrieving it.

I walked back and forth along the sandbar in sheer disbelief. To have come so far and be undone but such a stupid mistake—it was the epitome of frustration, but at the same time, stupidity is what brought me out here in the first place. Occasionally, a fit of desperation would seize me and I would fix upon a crazy solution. Should I swim west? Could I set the kayak on fire? Could I use the kayak like a surfboard and paddle with my hands?

These solutions didn't get me far. I had just about worn a track in the sandbar from my pacing when everything seemed to get louder and quieter at the same time. I fell to the sand, and curled up in a foetal position. I was overwhelmed by reality, ravenously hungry, my head was pounding and in my desperation, all I could think of was all the mistakes I had made up to this point.

I don't know how long I lay there. The water rippled and splashed, and the wind ruffled my hair. I remembered the earlier feeling of being the only person on earth and felt like that again, underscored by the lack of any other living creatures in visual range. The birds were long gone, there was no friendly dolphin to keep my spirits up. Even the indignant crab from my failed fishing attempt would have been something.

Eventually, the world around me started to darken and I was too demoralised to even look to see if it was nightfall or another storm. Either way, I lacked the energy and motivation to move. Night fell around me, not a cloud anywhere visible. My face itched and burned from the sun and the sand was rough under my skin, but even that was not enough to make me move. At some point, I must have slept because I opened my eyes to the predawn light of yet another day.

Hopelessness had me firmly in its grasp. I didn't know or care what the day would bring. I had long given up hope of a helicopter or ship—in fact, I had stopped even watching for ships. I lay on the sand amidst the pieces of my soul and pictured my family.

My beloved, handsome and rugged, skilled at outdoorsy things and always able to fix anything that broke. I had loved him since the day I met him. My daughter, who I completely believed was capable of ruling the world, in my biassed parental view. Creative and free-spirited, able to commune with any animal and a fountain of knowledge about the natural world. I would have given up anything to see them one final time. I had no tears left to cry, and my heart was so broken and beat that I wasn't grieving or raging. I simply was, and I was waiting to not be.

I expected that hunger or thirst would finish me, and somewhere in my haze, I realized I had not had anything to drink in an excessively long time. I knew there were two bottles on the kayak full of fresh rainwater, but still, I didn't move. Dehydration would hopefully take me soon and end this foolish experience. I hoped that one day my kayak would be found and my family would know I fought for them as long as I could. Given the storm that had wiped out my careful arrow in such a short time, I didn't even see the point in scratching a note in the sand. My remains and my kayak would have to speak for themselves, if anyone ever managed to find them.

The day passed, the skin on my face and neck burning on the side facing up. Irritation started to creep in after many hours in the sun. I thought that dying of exposure was quicker than this. I couldn't understand how I was still staring at the horizon and experiencing thirst, hunger and pain.

Irritation provided sufficient distraction that I didn't acknowledge the noise at first. A buzzing, grinding sort of noise that seemed entirely out of place with the splashing of the waves. It was only when it continued and began to get louder that I was roused from my apathy.

Hours of no movement added to my thirst and malnutrition made it nearly impossible to lift my head. It took a great deal of energy to simply lift myself up enough to look for the source of the sound, and when I didn't see anything I dropped back to the sand, angry at myself for even caring. I lay on the burning sand and if I had been hydrated enough I might have cried. Instead, I stared at the grains of the sand directly in front of me.

The noise was getting louder and louder, and I wanted to shout at it to shut up and let me die in peace. My voice was long gone and so was my energy. I just closed my eyes and conjured up the faces of those I loved the most.

Soon this nightmare would be over.

Chapter 8: The End

I could hear voices, over and above the constant droning. Almost as if they were shouting at each other. Let them shout, I thought. I'm too tired to mediate. I was mentally drifting, I could feel the burning sand on my skin and the itch of the sunburn and the pain of hunger in my belly, but those things seemed far away. The voices were somewhere around me but also oddly muffled and distant. Nothing seemed to matter. I was just drifting in and out of reality. Occasionally, a flash, like a dream, would come to mind—my daughter, my husband, pleasant memories of times we had been out on the lake, our home, our dog.

I let the dreamy flashes come and go. I was beyond fear, and beyond pain. I was calm and ready to drift away completely. But the voices were interrupting my peace, harsh voices. Urgent voices. Something was wrong, somebody was hurt. They had to hurry. I wished them well. I hoped whoever was hurt would be okay. I wanted to say comforting things but the thoughts wouldn't turn into words. I felt myself drift one final time, this time into a soft, peaceful nothingness.

Then there was a shock of cold on my face. Something very cold, more so against the sunburn. I was confused. It pulled me out of the nothingness and suddenly the calm and the peace were gone and I was back on the sand in the searing hot sun. Disappointment flooded through me as reality made itself known most insistently. The cold would stop momentarily, and there was noise that I couldn't make out and then there would be more cold. It was nice and soothing on the sunburn but every time the cold splashed on my face I would also feel every sore muscle, every hunger pang, every beat of the blood pulsing through my temples. I tried weakly to turn my head away from the cold and the noise got louder.

Now, instead of cold, there was a pressure. Something was tapping my cheek, then a noise, then more tapping. Something was happening to my arms too but it was all confusing. I felt a sharp poke in my elbow as I started to drift again, and then the noises changed. Suddenly, there was a flurry of activity all around me. I could feel things moving me and touching me, and there were different noises that seemed to be communicating with one another. Some more cold touched my face and I heard very clearly a voice say, "It's alright now, love, we've got you. You're going to be okay."

I drifted once more.

Then there was a different kind of softness, like the sand had morphed into a bed. I was no longer being burned on hot sand under an even hotter sun, I was under shade and on something cool, soft and smooth. Something moved to the side of me, and instinctively, I moved my arm to defend myself only to find I couldn't. Something was against my wrist, holding my arm down. I started to panic, not understanding what was going on. A face appeared above me, and a different, softer voice told me to relax, that I was safe and they were taking me home.

Home!

That word cut through everything else. Suddenly, my situation came into sharp focus. I tried to sit up only to have my shoulders held down. The face appeared again. "You need to relax. You are okay. You're on board our boat, and we're going to take you to get some medical help so you can go home." The face was friendly, and reassuring. I focused on it. It was an older man, a stranger but he was not at all threatening. He was looking at me carefully. "Do you understand where you are?" he asked. I nodded weakly. "My name is Thomas. I need you to stay lying down, as relaxed as you can. We've got some fluids going into you, which should help you start to feel better. We'll be back to base soon." A grin split his face, and I couldn't help a small smile in response. "You sure made it tricky. It's taken us days to find you!"

I tried to talk, tried to tell him how silly I'd been and how lucky I was to be alive but I didn't have the strength. He looked concerned again. "Don't try to talk. You're terribly dehydrated, and very weak. Just rest, we've got you now."

The hours and days suddenly caught up with me and I began to cry tearlessly. "Hey now. There's a couple of people waiting at the base who are just desperate to see you. Just breathe, and try to stay calm. You're safe." I tried to breathe through my sobs. My family was waiting for me, and I would see them soon. Despite everything I was going to see them again. I focused my mind on inhaling and exhaling and blocked all other thoughts. Just breathe in, and out, and we'll be there soon. They've got me. I'm safe.

After what was somehow the longest and shortest trip of my life, the boat started to slow. I could hear others yelling at each other, and Thomas leaned over to me. "We're coming into base now. It's going to be a bit bumpy as we lift you off, so just keep breathing and stay calm, ok? Let us do our job and take you to that ambulance so they can get you on your feet again." He grinned. "I can see a little blonde girl jumping up and down from here. She's been telling us for days that you'd be just fine, that if anyone could pull a miracle out of nowhere it'd be you." I sniffled. I felt weak physically, breathing was about the limit of my ability but my heart warmed at the idea that my baby girl was within sight.

He wasn't wrong about it being a bit bumpy. The stretcher I was on was passed from person to person along a human chain to a waiting ambulance. I couldn't see much except blue sky and after my misadventure, I wasn't sure I wanted to see much more of that but then the sweetest sound of all reached my ears.

"MAMA!!"

I could hear someone cautioning her to be gentle with me, and I could hear my husband's voice reassuring her that I was on land now, I was safe, and that once the paramedics had checked me out she could give me a hug. I didn't want to wait. I lifted my free arm and reached toward the sound, and her face came into view. Tearstreaked, dirty and unkempt, the poor darling looked as if she hadn't slept in days. My husband's face joined hers, and he looked worse. I wanted to say how sorry I was, how foolish and unthinking it had been to paddle away from them but I still didn't have the strength to speak. My husband leaned down and gently kissed me. "I am so glad to see you," he said through a teary smile.

A few days later, I was recuperating in hospital when Thomas poked his head into my room. He flashed me a grin and told me I was looking much better. All of the eloquent words of gratitude I had planned vanished, and all I could do was whisper "thank you." He told me how I'd been spotted by a search plane doing a flyover, how the helicopters and boats had searched fruitlessly in their projected search area but there had been no sign of me, and so out of desperation they had sent up a plane to see if my blue kayak could be spotted. They had seen me the afternoon before I was rescued but then the storm had rolled in and getting a boat out to me had to be delayed. They were afraid they were too late initially but once they got to me it was clear they were in fact just in time.

He grinned again as he told me they'd even managed to bring the kayak home. I wasn't sure I ever wanted to see it again but I was touched by the effort they had gone to on my behalf.

I thanked him again and again and asked him to pass my thanks on to everyone else involved. He grew serious and said that he was pleased the effort had such a positive outcome. I was being discharged the following day and other than some sunburn and weight loss I had suffered no permanent ill effects.

It's been a long time since that all happened, and my husband and daughter still go out on their kayaks but stick to lakes and inland rivers now. I haven't been back on my kayak yet, we replaced the paddle and it's been patiently waiting for me in the shed. The weather is shaping up to be pretty nice today, and I hear the reserve near the dam is looking pretty good. Out the window, I can see an expanse of cloudless blue sky.

I think it's about time we pack the waterproof bags with water, torches, sunscreen, protein balls and anything else that'll fit, and get back on the water.

It's going to be a beautiful afternoon.